The Essential Pirate Joke Book

J.A. Faust

Copyright © 2009 by J.A. Faust

All rights reserved.

No part of this book may be reproduced in any form or by any electronic or mechanical means, or the facilitation thereof, including information storage and retrieval systems, without permission in writing from the publisher, except the reviewer, who may quote brief passages for a review.

Any resemblance to actual persons, living or dead, events or locales is entirely coincidental.

Published in the United States by Lulu publishing.

www.Lulu.com

ISBN 978-0-557-07254-5

Introduction..4

Chapter 1: Aarrrguably the Best Pirate Jokes...........7

Chapter 2: Famous Pirate Jokes 28

Chapter 3: A Thirteen-Year-Old's Favorite Pirate Joke...34

Chapter 4: Pirate Star Jokes..............................35

Chapter 5: Obscure Pirate Jokes........................37

Chapter 6: A Pirate Walks into a Baarrr 40

Chapter 7: Writing Pirate Jokes for Fun and Profit..44

Appendix: Recommended Readings 46

Introduction

This entire book is written on one basic premise: Pirates love to say "Aarrr." To most people this probably seems like insufficient material to write an entire book. They're probably right. After reading this book you'll most likely wish you kept an eye on your receipt. But your receipt is gone now, taken by gnomes (gnomes are the pirates of domestic mythological creatures). But there are a few people out there who just can't get enough pirate jokes and this book is for them. People love lawyer jokes and pirates are really just more straight forward lawyers. Anyway the market for this book is people with a huge tolerance for redundancy and pirates. Pirates not because they want to know why people think they're funny; rather they'll force people to listen to the jokes as a form of ironic torture. This type of torture has become a preferred method because it's harder to prove damages, which is important in this age of lawyers. Once I was tied up and forced to listen to the collected works of Ann Rice. Of course this type of torture is ineffective if the person happens to like redundancy or terrible vampire fiction. If you are in the minority of people who don't skip introductions, you're probably regretting not skipping this one. So go ahead and skip to the jokes. I know what you're thinking "But the introduction isn't over yet!" But it really is, I'm just going to repeat everything in order to drive home the point that this book is really redundant. This entire book is written on one basic premise: Pirates love to say "Aarrr." To most people this probably seems like insufficient material to write an entire book. They're probably right. After reading this book you'll most likely wish you kept an eye on your receipt. But your receipt is gone now, taken by gnomes (gnomes are the pirates of domestic mythological creatures). But there are a few people out there who just can't get enough pirate jokes and this book is for them. People love lawyer jokes and pirates are really just more straight forward lawyers. Anyway the market for this book is people with a huge tolerance for redundancy and pirates. Pirates not because they want to know why people think they're funny; rather they'll force people to listen to the jokes as a form of ironic torture. This type of torture has become a preferred method because it's harder to prove damages, which is important in this age of lawyers. Once I was tied up and forced to listen to the collected works of Ann Rice. Of course this type of torture is ineffective if the person happens to like redundancy or terrible vampire fiction. If you are in the minority of people who don't skip introductions, you're probably regretting not skipping this one. So go ahead and skip to the jokes. I know what you're thinking "But the introduction isn't over yet!" But it really is, I'm just going to repeat everything in order to drive home the point that this book is really redundant. This entire book is written on one basic premise: Pirates love to say "Aarrr." To most people...

Chapter 1: Aarrrguably the Best Pirate Jokes

What did the pirate steal?
> Aarrrt

What did the pirate hit in golf?
> Paarrr

What are pirates afraid of?
> Shaarrrks

How dangerous are pirates?
> It vaarrries

Why was the pirate cold?
> He was at the Aarrctic

What did the pirate say to his ex-girlfriend?
> You broke my heaarrrt

What do pirates use to defend themselves?
> Aarrrmor

Why did the pirate go back to jail?
> He violated his paarrrole

What's a pirate's favorite sport?
> Nascaarrr

What is a pirate's favorite candy bar?
> Claarrrk Baarrr (*double whammy!*)

What do pirates hate to get stuck in?
> Taarrr

Where do pirates keep their treasure?
> In caarrrgo

Where do pirates go to be entertained?
> An aarrrena

What do you call an official pirate?
> A caarrrd caarrrying pirate

Female pirates hate what?
> Taarrrantulas

What do pirates rest in?
> Aarrrmchairs

Why did the pirate have to retire?
> He developed caarrrpal tunnel syndrome

How do pirates like their ham?
> Caarrrved

Why did the pirate ship look so good?
> They used vaarrrnish

What are pirates often considered?
> Baarrrbaarrric

Where can you always find pirates?
> Maarrrinas

Why couldn't the young pirate get into the club?
> He was caarrrded

Where do pirates keep their weapons?
> In an aarrrsenal

Where do pirates walk their dogs?
> In the paarrrk

What is a pirate's favorite type of dog?
> A shaarrrpie

Where do young pirates go to have fun?
> A caarrrnival

What would you call an old pirate weapon?
> Aarrrtifacts

What do pirates like to eat?
> Baarrrbecue

Why have pirates never attacked Olathe, Kansas?

    It's too faarrr inshore

When is the best time to be a pirate?

    In waarrrs

On a pirate ship usually only the captain had an individual room. The other pirates had cramped shared quarters (that is to say, quaarrrters). Sometimes they didn't even have beds. Do you know where pirates preferred to sleep if they didn't have a proper bed?

    On the caarrrpet

Where do pirates keep fresh water?

    In jaarrrs

How do pirates tend to ride horses?

    Baarrreback

Where do pirates keep their food?

    In baarrrels

How do pirates measure the size of their ship?

    In yaarrrds

Why did the pirate boy fail math?
    He didn't know logaarrrithms

Why did the pirate boy fail English?
    He was caught plagiaarrrizing

How do pirates keep in shape?
    They use baarrrbells

What is a pirate's favorite holiday?
    New Yeaarrrs

What did the pirate send his mom on Mother's day?
    A caarrrd

What is a pirate's favorite National Monument?
    The Gateway Aarrrch

In order to pull off a raid a pirate must be what?
    Daarrring

What is the best school for pirates to go to?
    Haarrrvard

Why couldn't the pirates raid the town?
> It had a baarrrier

What did the fat pirate cut out of his diet?
> Laarrrd

How did the pirate know the future?
> By using taarrrot cards

People tend to mistakenly think a pirate's lifestyle is what?
> Caarrrefree

Why can't many people be pirates?
> It's haarrrd work

What kind of ships do pirates like to raid?
> Baarrrages

What kind of swords do pirates prefer?
> Laarrrge ones

What types of knives do pirates prefer?
> Shaarrrp ones

How did Victorian pirates get around on shore?
> In caarrriages

Why do pirates take flight after a raid?
> To avoid being aarrrested

Where do pirates thrive?
> In the Caarrribbean

How do you find out about famous pirates?
> Go to the aarrrchives

What did the pirate want on his burger?
> Cheddaarrr

What do pirates tend to throw over the side of their ship?
> Gaarrrbage

Where do geek pirates hang out?
> In aarrrcades

What do you call a geek pirate?
> A squaarrre

What is a pirate's favorite bird?
> The paarrrot

What do pirates watch on TV?
> Caarrrtoons

What's a pirate's favorite game?
> Daarrrts

Who are pirate enemies?
> Aarrrmed Forces

Where do pirates get their supplies?
> In the maarrrketplace

What is a pirate's favorite baseball team?
> The Pirates (*duh…*)

How was the pirate captured?
> There was a naarrrc

When do pirates prefer to attack?
> When it's daarrrk

What do pirates wear?
> Gaarrrments

What gives pirates a bad name?
> All the caarrrnage

What do pirates write with?
> Maarrrkers

Why do dogs annoy pirates?
> Because of their baarrrking

What musical instrument do pirates play?
> The Haarrrp

Why do pirates love Captain Crunch?
> It's paarrrt of a complete breakfast

Why don't pirates own homes?
> They hate doing yaarrrd work

Why don't pirates attack whalers?
> They have haarrrpoons

What type of pollution concerns pirates?
> Caarrrbon monoxide

Are there pirate kings?
> No, pirates are egalitaarrrian

What do pirates get on their pizzas?
> Aarrrtichokes

What do pirates make bets on?
> Maarrrch Madness

When they don't have weapons, what do pirates use in an attack?
> Kaarrrate

Why did the crew dislike the pirate captain?
> He was aarrrogant

A pirate's diet consists of plenty of what?
> Caarrrbohydrates

Where did the pirate keep his boat?
> In the haarrrbor

What do pirate boys play?
> Maarrrbles

What do pirates keep for luck?
> Chaarrrms

Who do pirates prefer to rob?
> The aarrristocracy

What do you call it when a pirate robs you?
> Laarrrceny

What happened to the pirate who couldn't get back to the ship on time?
> He was maarrrooned

Why did the pirates go to New Orleans?
> For Maarrrti Gras

What is a pirate's favorite mythological tale?
> Jason and the Aarrrgonauts

Where do pirates go on vacation?
> Aarrrgentina

Pirates like to drink what?

    Sarsapaarrrilla

Where do pirates keep their motorcycles?

    In gaarrrages (Yes, motorcycles are the preferred method of terrestrial transportation for pirates and other villainous seafarers.)

What kind of motorcycles to pirates ride?

    Haarrrley Davidson

What do you call a group of pirate ships?

    An aarrrmada

What do pirates do between raids?

    They play caarrrds

If pirates theoretically live underground, with the gnomes, rather than on the high seas, what would they raid?

    Quaarrries

The concept of "the noble pirate" is what?

    A paarrradox

What did the stylish pirate wear?
> Aarrrmani

Why do people flee from pirates?
> To get out of haarrrms way

Where do pirates get their food from?
> A faarrrm

Why did the pirate go to jail?
> For aarrrson

Pirates hate to crash their ship, but what do they love to crash?
> Paarrrties

What is a pirate's favorite field sport?
> Aarrchery

Where are there few pirates?
> The Aarrrabian Desert

How do pirates conserve energy?
> They caarrrpool

What is good training for a pirate?
> Aarrrmy training

In the treacherous world of a pirate it can be good to be what?
> Paarrranoid

What do pirates do in the winter?
> Snow boaarrrd

Where did the hillbilly pirate come from?
> Aarrrkansas

What did the pirate give to his sweetheart?
> A caarrrnation

How do pirates keep warm in the winter?
> With a paarrrka

What do pirates steal?
> Dollaarrrs

Why couldn't the pirates raid the ship?
> It had too many guaarrrds

Where's a good place to find a pirate?
> Baarrrbados

What is the lamest pirate hobby?
> Gaarrrdening

What are the chances of being raided by pirates today?
> It raarrrely happens

How do pirates keep track of the passage of time?
> With a calendaarrr

Can pirates travel fast?
> They can go waarrrp speed

What do pirates do when they are running low on food?
> They catch some caarrrp

What did the pirate use to protect his ship?
> A taarrrp

Where do rich pirates like to visit?
> Maarrrtha's Vineyaarrrd

Are gnome pirates real?
> They're imaginaarrry

What do pirates keep as pets?
> Caarrribou

Pirates are expected to be on the rise in the event of what?
> Aarrmageddon

What is a pirate's favorite restaurant?
> Long John Silver's

What can get stuck on the side of a pirate's ship?
> Baarrrnacles

Who builds pirate ships?
> Caarrrpenters

What do pirates read every morning?
> Gaarrrfield

What basketball team to pirates support?
> The Haarrrlem Globetrotters

What do pirates eat as snacks?
> Maarrrshmallows

Where do pirates go mountaineering?
> The Caarrrpathians

Why can't pirate ships go through the Straits of Magellan?
> It's too naarrrow

What do hip pirates wear?
> Eaarrrrings

What do pirates do to improve their vision?
> They eat caarrrots

To be effective pirates need to be seen as what?
> Scaarrry

What often causes pirates to give up their professions?
> Becoming paarrrents

What do pirates order at a pub?
> Maarrrgaritas

How do we know about ancient pirates?
> From aarrrchaeology

Pirates tend to be relatively unaffected by what natural disaster?
> Eaarrrthquakes

What did the grateful Japanese pirate say?
> Aarrrigato

What did the pirate doctor say to his patient?
> Open wide and say "Aarrr"

How do pirates like their steaks?
> Chaarrred

What does a pirate call his wife?
> Daarrrling

Why don't pirates drive cars?
> They can't paarrrallel paarrrk

What do you call a Russian Pirate captain?
> Czaarrr

Why are pirates hard to understand?
>	Because of all their jaarrrgon

What do you call a smart pirate?
>	A scholaarrr

Why couldn't the pirate move?
>	He was paarrralyzed

What are pirate clothes made of?
>	Yaarrrn

Where do pirates keep their clothes?
>	An aarrrmoire

Why was the pirate so ugly?
>	He was covered with waarrrts

What weapon did ancient pirates use?
>	Speaarrrs

Why did the pirate buy a new ship?
>	It was a baarrrgain

Where does a pirate go for medicine?
> A phaarrrmacist

Why did the pirate boy get in trouble in school?
> He wouldn't shaarrre with others

What did the lenient police do with the captured pirates?
> Gave them a waarrrning

What should you do if you are interested in becoming a pirate?
> Reseaarrrch the possibility

Where can you research about pirates?
> The libraarrry

Why should anyone become a pirate?
> There's good profit maarrrgins

Chapter 2:
Famous Pirate Jokes

Who is a pirate's favorite magician?
    Haarrry Potter

Who is a pirate's favorite Laker?
    Kaarrreem Abdul Jabbaarrr

What philosopher's teachings do pirates live by?
    Aarrristotle

What is a pirate's favorite comic book movie?
    The Daarrrk Knight

Who is a pirate's favorite stand up comedian?
    Demetri Maarrrtin

What is a pirate's favorite cartoon movie?

> The Caarrre Beaarrrs Movie (Surprising, right? They really connect with Funshine Bear.)

What is a pirate's favorite action movie?
> Chaarrrlie's Angels

Favorite Charlie's Angel?
> Drew Baarrrymore

Who is a pirate's favorite rocker?
> Dave Navaarrro

Who is a pirate's favorite US president?
> Jimmy Caarrrter

What is a pirate's favorite dark comedy?
> Faarrrgo

Who is a pirate's favorite cartoon character?
> Baarrrt Simpson (Maarrrge is a close second)

Who is a pirate's favorite tabloid personality?
> Tonya Haarrrding

Pirates surprisingly enjoy the music of whom?
    Baarrrbra Streisand

Who is a pirate's favorite Beatle?
    George Haarrrison

What is a pirate's favorite classic sci-fi film?
    Waarrr of the Worlds

Who is a pirate's favorite economist?
Kaarrrl Maarrrx

Who is a pirate's favorite female comedian?
    Jeneane Gaarrrofalo

Who is a pirate's favorite action hero?
    Arnold Schwaarrrzenegger

Who is a pirate's favorite Academy Award winning actress?
    Hillaarrry Swank

What is a pirate's favorite fantasy movie?
    The Chronicles of Naarrrnia

How do pirates know the rest of the story?
> From Paul Haarrrvey

Who is a pirate's favorite comic actor?
> Jim Caarrrey

What is a pirate's favorite sitcom?
> Aarrrested Development

What is a pirate's favorite British drama?
> Daarrrk Shadows

Who is a pirate's favorite perpetual film bad guy?
> Gaarrry Sinise

Who is a pirate's favorite actress?
> Shaarrron Stone

Who is a pirate's favorite overall actor?
> Haarrrison Ford

Who is a pirate's favorite evil film character?
> Daarrrth Vader

Who is a pirate's favorite country singer?
    Dolly Paarrrton

Who is a pirate's favorite artist?
    Andy Waarrrhol

Who is a pirate's favorite reggae musician?
    Bob Maarrrley

What is a pirate's favorite cult movie?
    The Waarrriors

Who is a pirate's favorite scientist?
    Daarrrwin

Who do pirates get their news from?
    Larrry King

Why do pirates have such nice ships?
    They watch Maarrrtha Stewaarrrd

What is a pirate's favorite pop band?
    Paarrramore

Who do pirates go to for help with vampires?

    Saarrrah Michelle Gellaarrr

Who is a pirate's favorite member of Simon and Garfunkel?

    I'm sorry but you're going to have to figure this one out on your own. I can't be holding your hand forever.

Chapter 3: A Thirteen Year Old's Favorite Pirate Joke

Why did the pirates leave the room?
    Somebody faarrrted

Chapter 4: Pirate Star Jokes

Because the editors of this book couldn't decide which pirate star joke was the best, we decided to give you all of them.

How does a pirate navigate?
> By observing the staarrrs

What do pirates call the right side of a ship?
> Staarrrboaarrrd

What do pirates do in Hollywood?
> Go to homes of the Staarrrs

What's a pirate's favorite movie?
> Staarrr Waarrrs

How did Blackbeard become a famous pirate?
    He was on Staarrr Search

What candy do pirates like?
    Staarrrbursts

How do pirates start their day?
    With coffee from Staarrrbucks

Which Decepticon do pirates like?
    Staarrrscream

What band do pirates use for karaoke?
    Staarrrland Vocal Band

What video game do pirates play?
    Staarrr Fox

What are pirates easily impressed by?
    Guest Staarrrs

Chapter 5: Obscure Pirate Jokes

Why could pirates do whatever they wanted?
    Their captain gave them caarrrte blanche

How do pirates get past the Valluga Mountains?
    They take the Aarrrlberg Tunnel

What noble gas do museum curators use to protect antique pirate materials from oxidation?
    Aarrrgon

How do pirates conduct raids on the interior of Columbia or Venezuela?
    They take the Aarrruca River

What did ancient Greek pirates call their captain?
> Aarrrchon

Why did the pirates avoid Brazil?
> They're afraid of the jaarrracasas monster

What did the pirates from the New Ireland Province of Papua New Guinea speak?
> Kaarrra

Pirates like to wear the pelt of what Asian sheep?
> The kaarrrakul

What port do Pirates use in Greenland?
> Naarrrsaarrrsuaq

What do Celtic pirates do for entertainment?
> They kidnap a baarrrd

What town in northern France did the pirates raid?
> Aarrras

What large heavy knife did Malaysian pirates use?
> A paarrrang

What was the name of the small quick sailing ships used by Portuguese pirates in the fifteenth century?

    The caarrravel

Pirates respected what Native American tribe from present day Rode Island?

    The Naarrragansett

What surrealist author do Japanese pirates read?

    Haarrruki Murakami

What do pirates call the number of objects in a set?

    Caarrrdinality

What did pirates use for lighting in the late eighteenth century?

    An aarrrgand lamp

Chapter 6: A Pirate Walks into a Baarrr...

The author of this book decided to add this collection of the best pirate bar jokes around as a way of saying "Please don't hunt me down for all the terrible 'aarrr' jokes."

A one eyed pirate walks into a bar. The bartender says "Hey, how did you decide to become a pirate?" The pirate replies "Well, I wanted to be a teacher, but I only had one pupil."

A green pirate walks into a bar. The bartender says "You're a strange looking pirate." The pirate replies "I'm from Maarrrs."

A one armed, one legged pirate walks into a bar. The bartender notices that the pirate's hook is made of silver and his peg leg is made of mahogany. The bartender says "That's a nice hook and peg." The pirate replies "Aarrr, they cost me an arm and a leg."

A pirate walks into a bar with a paper towel on his face. The bartender says "What's with the paper towel?" The pirate answers "Aarrr, I've got a bounty on me head."

A pirate with golden earrings walks into a bar. The bartender says "Hey, how much did those earrings cost you?" The pirate replies "Aarrr, they cost a buck-an-ear."

A one armed, one legged, one eyed pirate walks into a bar. The bartender says "You look terrible! What happened to your leg?" The pirate responds "I was taking a swim and a great white bit my leg clean off." The bartender gasped "How horrible! Did the shark bite your arm off as well?" "No," responded the pirate "I was boarding a ship and I lost my arm in a sword fight." Then the bartender asked "And what about your eye?" "A bird pooped in my eye." The pirate answered. Shocked, the bartender replied "You lost your eye from bird poop?" The pirate turned pale "Aarrr, I wasn't used to the hook yet."

41

A pirate walks into a bar with a steering wheel sticking out of the front of his pants. The bartender says "Why do you have a steering wheel?" The pirate responds "Aarrr, it drives me nuts."

Two pirates walk into a bar, the third one ducks.

A pirate, a ninja and a zombie walk into a bar. The bar explodes. No one place can hold that much awesome.

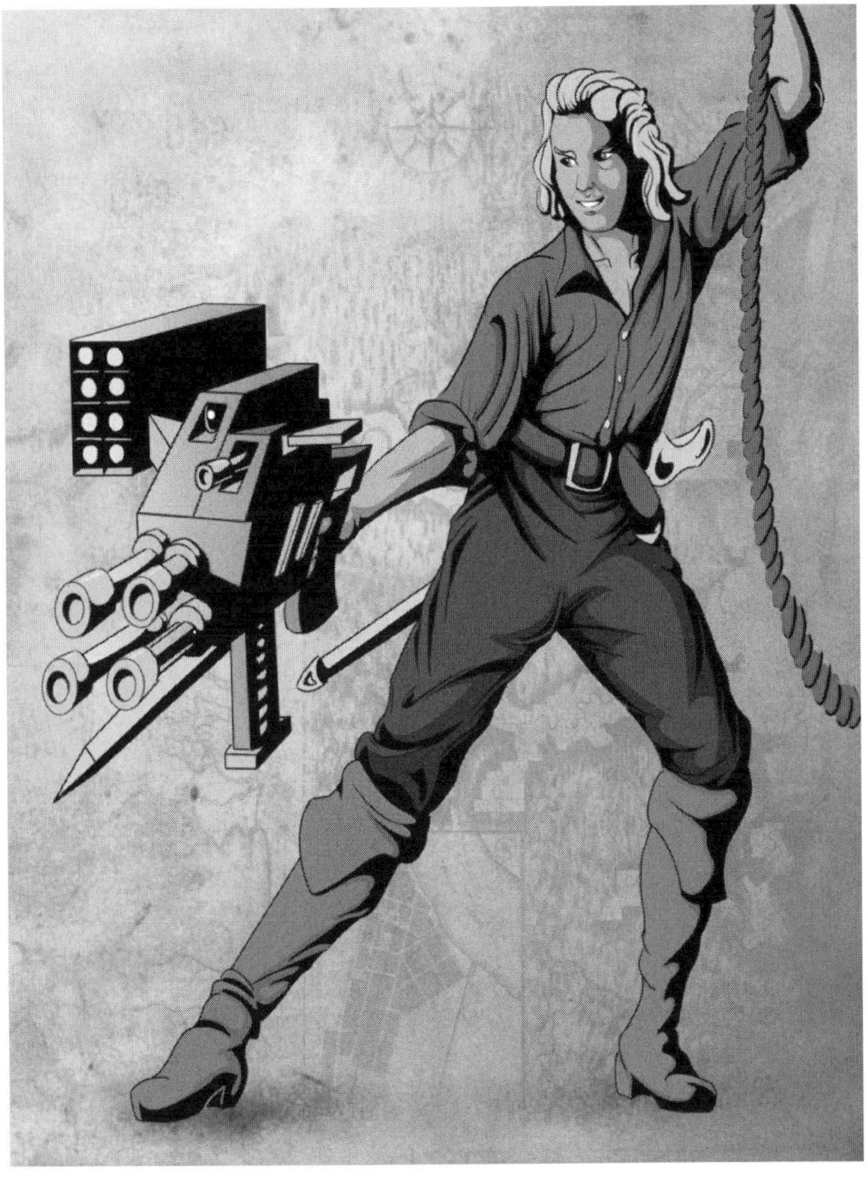

Chapter 7:
Writing Pirate Jokes for Fun and Profit

If you haven't figured it out by now, even gnomes could write pirate jokes if they had to. The most important thing is to have a word with an "ar" in it. Preferably a noun. It is pretty much downhill from there. Replace the "ar" with "aarrr."

Example: Fart → Faarrrt

Three letter R's is enough, a page full of R's doesn't make the joke funnier, just kind of hard to read. When doing the joke orally be sure to enunciate. All you need after that is a question with that relates to the "ar" word and includes the word pirate. Be sure to ask the question first or else it will just come off as sort of nonsensical.

Example:
>Why did the pirate call safety?
>He faarrrted

Don't give into the temptation to use "or" "er" or "air" instead of "ar." Besides, pirates wouldn't be coming down with scurvy all the time if their favorite fruit was oranges, so it's a stupid joke anyway.

You are now on your way to becoming a professional pirate joke writer. And chicks dig that[1]. But try to have a couple jokes that are not about farting. Grow up.

---

[1] That's a lie. Women do not dig funny men. They dig men better looking than you. Aarrr…

Appendix: Recommended Readings

The Great Big Pirate Joke Book

Uncle Herb's Pirate Joke Treasure Chest

The Dangerous Pirate Joke Book for Boys

The Pirate Joke Collection: Volume 1

The Pirate Joke Collection: Volume 2

The Pirate Joke Collection: Volume 3

The Pirate Joke Collection: Volume 5

How I Pulled Myself Out of the Gutter One Pirate Joke at a time: The J.A. Faust Story

Chicken Soup for the Pirate's Soul

Dummies Guide to being a Pirate

A Thousand Splendid Pirate Jokes

The Hardy Boys and the Secret Jokes of Pirate Cove

Pirates: the Myths, the Legends, the Hilarious Jokes

~~The Communist Manifesto~~

A Series of Unfortunate Pirate Jokes

Pirate Jokes Aarrre the Best

Printed in Great Britain
by Amazon